UNION BEACH SCHOOL LIBRARY

c.1 3/89 Set of 12 $119.40 Crestwood
($9.95)

CENTER STAGE

JULIAN LENNON

By
**William Sanford
Carl Green**

Edited By
Dr. Howard Schroeder
Professor in Reading and Language Arts
Dept. of Elementary Education
Mankato State University

Produced & Designed By
Baker Street Productions, Ltd.

CRESTWOOD HOUSE

Mankato, Minnesota
U.S.A.

LIBRARY OF CONGRESS CATALOGING IN PUBLICATION DATA

Sanford, William R. (William Reynolds), 1927 -
Julian Lennon.

(Center stage)
SUMMARY: Examines the life and musical career of the son of Beatle John Lennon and describes his efforts to escape his famous father's shadow and prove himself a recording artist in his own right.
  1. Lennon, Julian, 1963-   —Juvenile literature. 2. Rock musicians—Biography—Juvenile Literature. [1. Lennon, Julian, 1963-   . 2. Musicians. 3. Rock music] I. Green, Carl R. II Schroeder, Howard. III .Title. IV. Series.
ML3930.L35S26   1986   784.5'4'00924 [B]   86-8949
ISBN 0-89686-301-8

International Standard
Book Number:
0-89686-301-8

Library of Congress
Catalog Card Number:
86-8949

ILLUSTRATION CREDITS:

Cover: Scott Weiner/Retna
Ron Wolfson/LGI: 5, 10
Richard Pasley/LGI: 6
Brett Cochran/LGI: 9, 25
Patrick Harbron/LGI: 13
Wide World Photos: 15
Dave Hogan/LGI: 18, 26
Jeffrey Blake/LGI: 21
Nick Elgar/LGI: 22
Lynn Goldsmith/LGI: 29
Scott Weiner/Retna: 30-31, 32

Copyright© 1986 by Crestwood House, Inc. All rights reserved. No part of this book may be reproduced in any form without written permission from the publisher, except for brief passages included in a review. Printed in the United States of America.

Hwy. 66 South, Box 3427
Mankato, MN 56002-3427
507-388-1616

TABLE OF CONTENTS

Introduction
A new record brings back memories 4
Chapter I
There's never been another group like the Beatles . . 7
Too much pressure 8
Chapter II
"Who's going to be a famous rocker?" 9
A new home and a hit drawing 11
The family breaks up 12
School isn't easy 13
Growing up is hard to do 14
Julian's first record 14
A fatal shooting 15
Money problems 16
Chapter III
From playboy to top-flight musician 17
The first big chance 17
Turning songs into an album 19
A polished sound 20
A concert starts with rehearsals 21
A good-luck charm 23
Opening night of the tour 24
The critics approve 24
Chapter IV
Where does Julian go from here? 27
At home in London 28
Working on a new album 28

INTRODUCTION

A new record brings back memories

Disk jockeys began playing a new record late in 1984. People stopped to listen when they heard the music. The voice sounded strangely familiar.

"That's John Lennon!" some rock fans said. But no one could remember the famous Beatle singing those songs. Was this a "lost" album that John had recorded years ago? Or was someone trying to imitate John's voice? If so, it wouldn't be the first time. Other singers had tried to cash in on the love people felt for John Lennon.

Everyone knew that a madman killed John Lennon in 1980. Even so, this young tenor voice sounded just like John's. It had the same haunting sound. No one who heard it would have guessed that the singer was making his first record.

The music came from an album called *Valotte*. A look at the album cover soon explained the reason for the John Lennon sound. *Valotte's* composer and singer **was**

Julian Lennon has a sound that's very familiar.

a Lennon. It was the first album made by John Lennon's oldest son, Julian Lennon.

Many of John's fans were pleased that his sound was still alive. They liked the thought that Julian was carrying on his father's work. Others weren't so happy. Julian's critics said that he was imitating his father. No one, they said, should make money by taking advantage of John's name.

Julian isn't afraid to speak out. He answered his critics in these words: "When I open my mouth, that's what comes out. I'm not trying to copy anybody." As for being a Lennon, he says, "The name Lennon will open a door, but if they don't like you, they'll slam it in your face."

That's the reason Julian works so hard. People are always comparing him with the Beatles.

Julian wants to be known for his own ability.

CHAPTER ONE

There's never been another group like the Beatles

What's the name of the most popular rock group that ever cut a record? A few fans might vote for the Beach Boys or the Rolling Stones. But most rock music lovers know there's only one answer to that question: the Beatles.

The Beatles were more than a "hot" rock group. Their music will live forever—and Julian Lennon grew up with that music.

In 1961, John Lennon, George Harrison, Paul McCartney, and Pete Best started a rock band. Brian Epstein found them playing in a rock 'n' roll club in Liverpool, England. He thought they had some talent and took over as their manager. One of his first moves was to replace Pete with Ringo Starr. He also took away the group's leather jackets and gave them a clean-cut look.

The Beatles hit the big time almost at once. Their recording of *Please Please Me* became a number one hit in 1962. The song had a beat like thunder, a catchy tune, and rich harmonies. In February, 1963, the Beatles made their first album. John and Paul wrote the songs. The songs were so good that other singers begged for the chance to record them.

By the summer of 1963, the Beatles were moving fast. They starred on a popular radio show and made more hit records. The group followed their records to the United States in 1964. Fans caused a riot at the airport when the Beatles arrived. The boys appeared on television and made their first movie. Beatles songs took over the top four places on pop charts in the U.S.

Everything the Beatles did turned to gold. In 1965, Queen Elizabeth II gave them a special award for service to their country. Every one of their albums sold millions of copies. Young people dressed like their heroes and fought for tickets to Beatles' concerts.

Too much pressure

Despite their success, the pressures of the music business were too much for some of the Beatles. In 1967, John told reporters that the group wouldn't make any more tours. Three years later, they split up. Each of the Beatles went off to make his own music in his own way. Many people tried to talk them into playing together again, but they never did.

Those busy years didn't leave the Beatles much time for their families. Young Julian grew up with the group's music, but his father was gone much of the time.

CHAPTER TWO

"Who's going to be a famous rocker?"

In April of 1963, *Please Please Me* was riding high on the charts. Brian Epstein had big plans for Beatles albums and concert tours. Teenagers screamed and pushed and shouted out their love for the four Beatles.

John Charles Julian Lennon was born into that scene.

Julian was born April 8, 1963.

His birth didn't make the newspapers. The Beatles' managers didn't want the fans to know that John had married Cynthia Powell on August 23, 1962. The baby was born on April 8, 1963, in a Liverpool hospital. The parents named him "John" in honor of Cynthia's father. The "Julian" was for Julia, John Lennon's mother. John always called his son by that name.

The Beatles were on tour when Julian was born. John wore a disguise when he went to the hospital a week later. When he picked up the baby, John made a guess about the future. He asked his son, "Who's going to be a famous rocker like his dad?"

John Lennon guessed that his son, Julian, would be famous.

The Lennons moved to London that summer. The marriage was no longer a secret. When Cynthia took Julian out for a walk, fans crowded around. They wanted to look at "John's baby." John was too busy with recording dates and concerts to be a good father. He didn't help much when he was at home, either. When Cynthia changed Julian's diapers, John often left the room.

A new home and a hit drawing

By 1964, John was beginning to enjoy his success. The American tour was a hit, as was the Beatles' movie, *A Hard Day's Night*. John bought a home twenty miles outside of London. In that quiet setting, he found some peace. Julian remembers going shopping with his mother in a nearby town. John's fans stopped Cynthia on the street and gave her gifts for Julian.

When he was old enough, Julian went to school. Art was his best subject. One day he showed John his drawing of a girl with blonde hair. The sky behind her was filled with stars. Julian told his father that the picture was "Lucy in the sky." A little later, John turned the drawing into a hit song. He called it *Lucy in the Sky with Diamonds*. Another of Julian's pictures showed up on the cover of the *Christmas Time Is Here Again* album.

The family breaks up

The Lennons' marriage broke up in 1968. Cynthia asked for a divorce after John fell in love with an artist named Yoko Ono. After that, five-year-old Julian saw his father only on weekends. He says, "All I knew was that he was away a lot. When he came home and we were together, I recall most of all the fun, like . . . riding on the back of Dad's motorbike down to Ringo's home."

There weren't very many good times. Julian was often sad, a fact that helped inspire another popular Beatles record. Paul McCartney came by one day with a song he hoped would make the boy feel better. He called it *Hey Jude*. Jude was one of Julian's nicknames. One famous line said, "Hey Jude/don't make it bad/Take a sad song/and make it better." *Hey Jude* went on to become the best-selling Beatles song of all time.

In 1969, John married Yoko and moved to New York. After that, Julian only saw his father once or twice a year. One visit almost ended in tragedy. John and Yoko took Julian and Yoko's daughter, Kyoko, on a trip to Scotland. The vacation ended in a car crash that sent all four Lennons to the hospital.

School isn't easy

Life kept changing for Julian. His mother married again in 1970. Julian didn't like his stepfather. The marriage didn't last long, nor did a third marriage. School was also hard for the son of John Lennon. His classmates picked on him because they thought he was a spoiled rich kid. Julian learned to fight back—but not too hard. "You couldn't get too abusive, either, or it was no more front teeth, mate," he says.

Julian learned to play the guitar at school. He and a good friend, Justin Clayton, sometimes skipped classes to practice their music. It was clear that Julian wanted to follow in his father's footsteps. But did he have the talent?

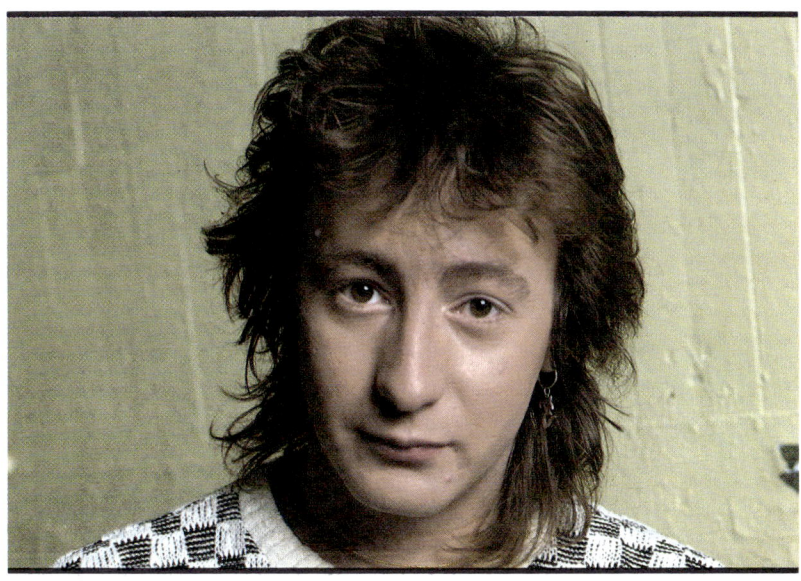

While in school, Julian decided he wanted to be a musician.

Growing up is hard to do

Growing up wasn't easy for Julian Lennon. His mother helped him as much as she could. She understood his moods and she let him see his father whenever John had time for the boy. As a result, Cynthia Lennon and her son are still very close.

Some of Julian's best memories come from 1973 and 1974. Julian saw his father more often in those years. John and Yoko's marriage was in trouble and they weren't living together. On one trip, father and son went to Disneyland. Another time, John took Julian to meet rock stars Elton John and Mick Jagger.

Julian's first record

John took eleven-year-old Julian to a recording studio one day in 1974. Julian kept time on the drums and John played the piano. Julian had been drumming since he was five, and he had a great time. The big surprise came when John told him that their jam session would be used on an album called *Walls and Bridges*. Julian told his father, "If I'd known it was going to be on the album, I would have played better."

After that, John went back to Yoko. In October, 1975,

Yoko gave birth to John's son, Sean Ono Lennon. Julian felt left out, because John paid so much attention to Sean. It hurt even more when John told a magazine that Julian's birth was an accident.

John didn't mean to be cruel. He said that Julian would always belong to him. John knew that being a Lennon would be hard on his oldest child. "Everyone has a cross to bear," he said, "and Julian has that cross, and he'll deal with it." Today, when he's asked about the painful things his father said, Julian replies, "Makes no difference. I love him and respect him, and I'm really proud of him."

A fatal shooting

Julian and John got along better when Julian became a teenager. When they met, they had a good time playing old rock songs together. In April, 1980, John gave his son a birthday party on his boat in Palm Beach, Florida. That was the last time Julian saw his father alive. On the night of December 8, 1980, Mark David Chapman shot John five times with a revolver.

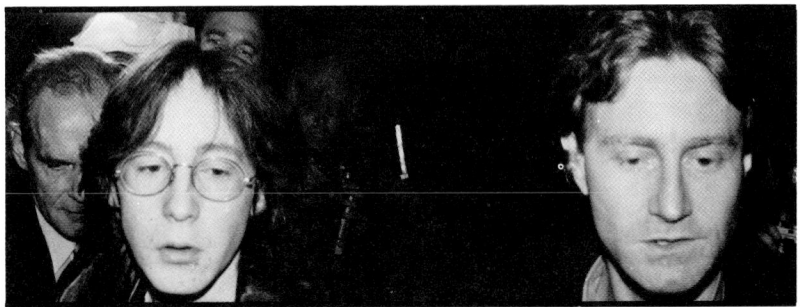

Julian went to New York to be with Yoko and Sean after his father's death.

Seventeen-year-old Julian flew to New York to be with Yoko and Sean. Despite his own sadness, he helped Sean mourn their father's death.

After John died, Julian's life fell apart for a while. He recalls that when he heard the news, "I wanted to hit and smash everything." He dropped out of school and moved to London. In London, he lived a wild life. The newspapers reported that he was drinking too much. At one point he dyed his hair blond. Julian also signed a bad contract. A producer wanted him to record a song that had been stolen from his father. Yoko helped Julian get out of the deal by paying $20,000 (US) to the producer.

Money problems

Julian's money problems also made news. Some reports said that he was broke and was washing dishes for a living. That seemed strange, because Yoko inherited over $100 million (US) from John. Julian didn't share in that fortune. John left him a $250,000 (US) trust fund, to be paid in 1989. But even though he wasn't rich, Julian didn't go hungry. Yoko gave him money to live on, and Cynthia bought him an apartment.

Handouts weren't Julian's style, however. Music was in his blood. Could he make it as a musician? The Lennon name would always sell records, but Julian wanted to be his own man. To make that happen, he began writing his own songs.

CHAPTER THREE

From playboy to top-flight musician

Once Julian decided to make a career in music, he buckled down to work. "Writing and singing were always great fun for me," he says. The long hours of practice began to pay off.

In 1983, Julian formed a group called Quasar. Julian played drums, and Justin Clayton played guitar. Julian hoped that three years after John's death no one would accuse him of using his father's name to get ahead. He was wrong. Record companies have long memories. Quasar couldn't land a contract.

The first big chance

Julian didn't give up. A friend named Dean Gordon heard his demo tapes. Dean didn't know much about the music business, but he signed on as Julian's manager. His job was to take the tapes around to the record companies. Despite his efforts, the big companies

Julian posed for this picture in 1983.

weren't buying. They didn't want the public to blame them for trying to make money from a John Lennon "clone."

Finally, a small company called Charisma offered Julian a contract. In return, Julian promised to put all his energy into his first album. Justin Clayton and Carlton (Carlos) Morales joined him. The three young musicians stayed at a big house in France. Valotte was a quiet place to work, far from the busy life of London.

Julian and his friends spent three months in France. They made demo tapes for a dozen songs. Ten of the songs later appeared on the album. Julian wrote or co-wrote nine of the ten songs. The work didn't always go smoothly. Julian and Justin argued much of the time. They each had different tastes in music. When the battles got too hot, Carlos stepped in as the peacemaker.

Turning songs into an album

For Julian, the album was a high point in his life. "I wanted to get it [the album] out of the way," he said. "I had these songs that were written from experience, things I had gone through. . . . Now that I've got it off my chest, I feel fine." But writing the songs was only the first step. Julian still had to record the music. He decided to call the album *Valotte*.

Julian talked Phil Ramone, a well-known producer,

into helping with the album. Phil became almost a second father to Julian. The producer started by hiring top-notch musicians. He brought in the Muscle Shoals Rhythm Section, harmonica player Toots Thielemans, and saxophonist Michael Breaker. Julian was shy around the older musicians. He learned quickly, however, and the recording went well. In addition to Julian's singing, the album shows off his skill on bass guitar, keyboards, and drums.

A polished sound

Most critics liked the music Julian wrote for *Valotte*. They said it sounded like the work of a much older musician. A few critics, however, said that Julian sang too much like John. They also complained that his song lyrics were "childish." The public disagreed. People liked what they heard. The album went "platinum" when its sales hit the one million mark. Two songs, *Too Late for Goodbyes* and *Valotte*, made the Top Ten on both sides of the Atlantic Ocean.

For all its polish, *Valotte's* songs are deeply personal. In *Well I Don't Know*, Julian sings, "I hear you, do you hear me?" The words tell us that Julian remembered something his father once told him. "After I'm dead," John said long ago, "look for a white feather floating across the room." Julian is still watching for the feather.

After *Valotte*, Atlantic Records signed Julian to his

first U.S. contract. Plans also were made for a six-week concert tour. "Jules," as some people call him, started getting nervous. He knew that singing in front of a live audience is the real test of a musician. In a studio, mistakes can be fixed. A live concert has to be right the first time.

A concert starts with rehearsals

The first concert was set for March, 1985, in San Antonio, Texas. With *Valotte* doing so well, the concert sold out in two hours. Rehearsals came next. Dean Gordon brought in some fine musicians to play backup for Julian. Justin Clayton was there, too.

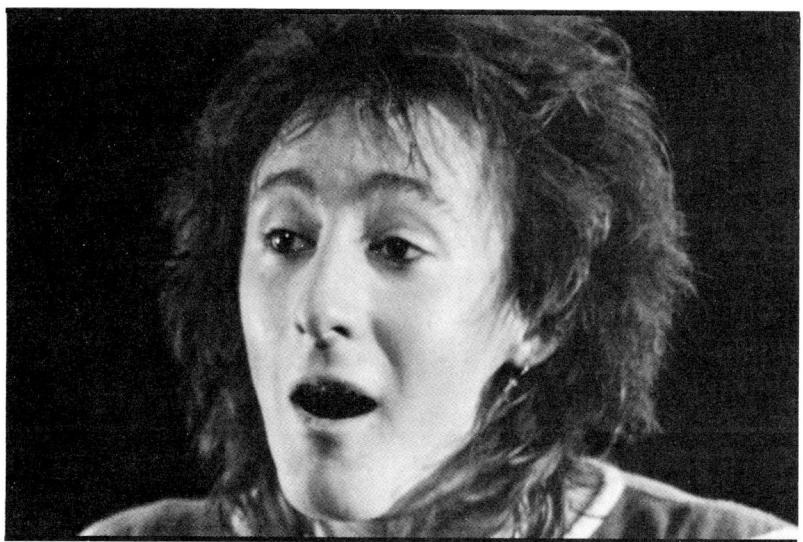

Julian's first concert would be in San Antonio, Texas.

The band flew into Dallas, Texas, for rehearsals. The huge rehearsal hall made Julian even more nervous. He pretended to cry. "I want me mummy. I want to go home," he said. Someone told him that it was too late for that. Julian smiled and said quietly, "I know." Starting the rehearsals helped him relax. Between songs, he rode his skateboard around the empty hall.

Later, Julian watched a video of the first rehearsal. He wasn't happy with what he saw. It wasn't his looks that upset him. He knows his pale, sharp features aren't movie-star handsome. Instead, he saw himself walking

Julian worked hard during rehearsals for his U.S. tour.

around in circles while he was singing. As the days went on, however, he took command. Soon he was strutting around like he owned the stage.

A good-luck charm

After rehearsals one night, Julian told the musicians to wear socks of different colors. He thought the mixed socks would bring them good luck. The next day, Julian wore one black sock and one white sock. From then on, he checked every day to make sure the band was following orders.

Julian had very few free moments during the two weeks of rehearsals. Reporters followed him everywhere he went in Dallas. Crowds of teenage girls waited outside the hall each day. Julian didn't get upset at the demand for interviews and autographs. He knows that rock stars owe their careers to the public.

The concert began to take shape. Some of Julian's clowning around became part of the act. Toward the end of rehearsals, Julian caught a cold. He worried about losing his voice, but his luck stayed good.

Finally, it was time for the dress rehearsal. A small audience had been invited so that Julian could perform in front of a live crowd. The sight of the audience gave Julian a bad case of stage fright. The attack of nerves didn't last long, however. When the time came, he ran onto the stage and began singing his first number. The audience loved him.

Opening night of the tour

The band left for San Antonio that night. On the bus, Julian laughed about the dress rehearsal. He knew he'd hit some wrong notes. In addition, he sang the second chorus of *Valotte* instead of the first. But he'd passed his first big test.

Julian was nervous all over again the next night. The sound of a big audience waiting to hear him sing was new to him. To calm his nerves, he did some pushups. Finally, the concert started. By the end of the third song, Julian was relaxed enough to talk to his fans. The crowd broke into wild applause and people threw roses onto the stage.

The critics approve

The newspapers praised the concert. One critic wrote, "... a powerful concert debut that left little doubt the son of the late John Lennon is his own man." Cynthia Lennon added her own review: "I was so thrilled that

Julian's U.S. tour was a big success.

Julian was Julian. He really is his own person. When he's on stage, he's nothing like John.''

Julian's concerts sold out in city after city. With each show, he became more confident. On stage, he laughed and clowned and had a good time. Off stage, he began to look toward the future.

Julian Lennon is pictured with his mother, Cynthia (on left), and a friend of hers.

CHAPTER FOUR

Where does Julian go from here?

Julian Lennon will never forget 1985. It was the year of his first album and his first concerts. Wherever he went, fans turned out with signs that read, "We love you, Julian!"

MCA Home Video joined in with a video called *Stand By Me, A Portrait of Julian Lennon*. The video shows scenes from Julian's concert tour. Julian told the camera crew to film him exactly as he is. "It shows me as silly, boring, and nervous," he said. "I wasn't holding anything back. . . . Generally I'm a home person. I like to sit at the piano and fiddle around.

The 1985 Grammy Awards were another big event for Julian. In February, he was nominated as Best New Artist of 1985. That was important, because Grammies mean the same to musicians as Oscars mean to film stars. This time, Julian's lucky socks didn't work. A beautiful singer named Sade won the Grammy for Best New Artist.

Julian wasn't too upset. He had already won the *Rolling Stone* award as best new male pop singer of

1985. The magazine's readers gave him almost as many votes as everyone else put together.

At home in London

Whenever possible, Julian spends time with his friends. "You've got to have the crowds around because this is a business," he explains. "But . . . I'm meeting so many people that I don't really know. That's when I need the closeness of real friends."

Julian isn't in any rush to grow up. He has a girlfriend, but he doesn't seem ready to get married. In fact, he still dresses like a teenager. He's usually seen wearing blue jeans with a T-shirt and sneakers. An earring hangs from his left ear, half-hidden by his long brown hair. Julian could buy a Rolls Royce, but he prefers to drive a tiny 1957 sports car.

Working on a new album

After *Valotte,* critics and fans looked forward to Julian's second album. He knew that many people thought he would be a one-album "wonder boy." To silence them, he put out *The Secret Value of Daydreaming* in May, 1986. Julian says the album is "more uptempo, but it still has some nice ballads." The new

Sean and Julian Lennon are pictured at a 1986 Rock and Roll Hall of Fame dinner with Billy Joel.

Julian checks his appearance before a photo session.

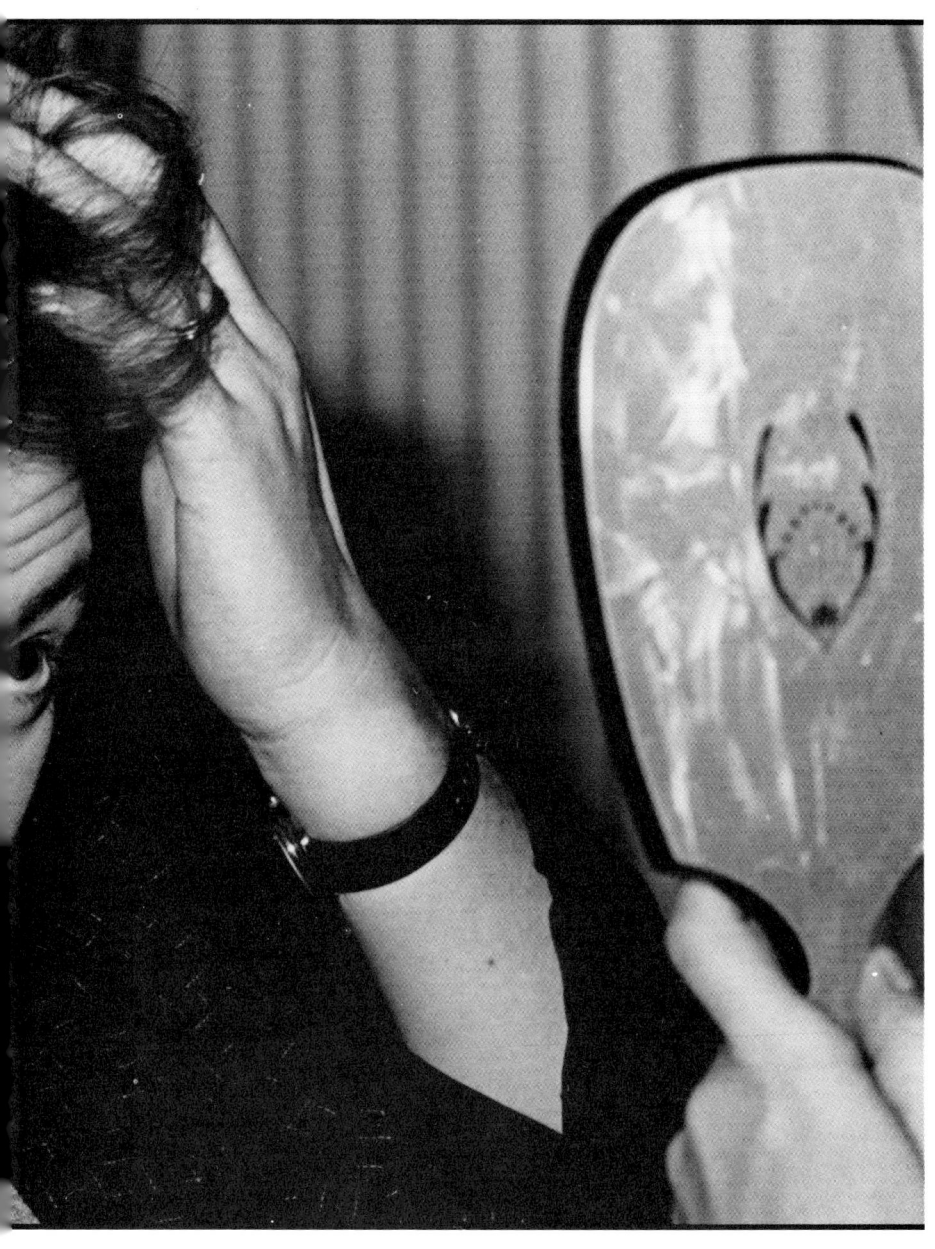

record shot upward on the charts after its release in May, 1986. Julian's fans particularly liked *Stick Around,* the album's hit single.

Julian knows how important the new album is to his career. "I haven't really secured anything for myself by having a hit record," he said. "If this second album doesn't make it, then I'm back on my backside again." But Julian doesn't look worried.

The singer's new confidence also shows when people ask him, "Would your father like what you're doing?" These days, Julian has a ready answer. "I hope so," he replies. "I'm writing music and performing. Why wouldn't he?"

Julian has a new confidence.